Joy

Hush, my little one, listen, Christmas bells are ringing,
Like the stars, how they glisten,
Ringing and singing and bringing in Christmas,
Hush, my little one, listen, the bells are ringing for you.

ANNE GEDDES

Christmas Joy

**Andrews McMeel
Publishing, LLC**

Kansas City

Christmas Comes From the Heart

Christmas comes from the heart
and has from the very start.
It's not about the gifts
but the spirits that we lift.
It's not about me but it is about you
and about all of the little children too.
It's about the love
that comes from all around including above.
It's about hope and peace
both of which never cease.
It's about a child's smile
that seems to go on for miles.
Christmas comes from the heart...

Eugenia Struchen

Rudolph the Red-Nosed Reindeer

Rudolph the red-nosed reindeer
Had a very shiny nose
And if you ever saw it
You would even say it glows

All of the other reindeer
Used to laugh and call him names
They never let poor Rudolph
Join in any reindeer games

Then one foggy Christmas Eve
Santa came to say,
"Rudolph, with your nose so bright
Won't you guide my sleigh tonight?"

Then how the reindeer loved him
As they shouted out with glee,
"Rudolph the red-nosed reindeer
You'll go down in history!"

Johnny Marks

Christmas Eve Night

It's Christmas Eve night
And the snow's falling hard,
A blanket of white
Will soon spread o'er our yard.
We know in our hearts
That before break of day
The snow will be marked
With the tracks of a sleigh.

Your eyes will be closed
But you'll see in your dreams
A castle on clouds
Made of marshmallow creams,
And candy canes hanging
From stars way up high,
And sugar plum fairies
That dance in the sky.

Travis Brasell

From Our Happy Home

From our happy home
Through the world we roam
One week in all the year,
Making winter spring
With the joy we bring
For Christmas-tide is here.

Now the eastern star
Shines from afar
To light the poorest home;
Hearts warmer grow,
Gifts freely flow,
For Christmas-tide has come.

Louisa May Alcott (1832–1888)

'Twas the Night Before Christmas

'Twas the night before Christmas,
When all through the house
Not a creature was stirring,
Not even a mouse.
The stockings were hung
By the chimney with care,
In hopes that St. Nicholas
Soon would be there.

The children were nestled
All snug in their beds,
While visions of sugar plums
Danced in their heads.
And mamma in her 'kerchief,
And I in my cap,
Had just settled our brains
For a long winter's nap.

Clement Clarke Moore (1779–1863)

O Christmas Tree

O Christmas tree, O Christmas tree!
How are thy leaves so verdant!
O Christmas tree, O Christmas tree,
How are thy leaves so verdant!
Not only in the summertime,
But even in winter is thy prime.
O Christmas tree, O Christmas tree,
How are thy leaves so verdant!

O Christmas tree, O Christmas tree,
Much pleasure doth thou bring me!
O Christmas tree, O Christmas tree,
Much pleasure doth thou bring me!
For every year the Christmas tree,
Brings to us all both joy and glee.
O Christmas tree, O Christmas tree,
Much pleasure doth thou bring me!

Jingle Bells

Dashing through the snow, on a one-horse open sleigh,
O'er the fields we go, laughing all the way;
Bells on bob-tail ring, making spirits bright,
What fun it is to ride and sing a sleighing song tonight!

Chorus
Jingle bells, jingle bells, jingle all the way!
O what fun it is to ride in a one-horse open sleigh.
Jingle bells, jingle bells, jingle all the way!
O what fun it is to ride in a one-horse open sleigh.

A day or two ago, I thought I'd take a ride,
And soon Miss Fanny Bright was seated by my side;
The horse was lean and lank, misfortune seemed his lot;
He got into a drifted bank and we got upsot.

James Pierpont (1822–1893)

Santa Claus is Coming to Town

You better watch out
You better not cry
Better not pout
I'm telling you why
Santa Claus is coming to town

He's making a list
And checking it twice
Gonna find out who's naughty and nice
Santa Claus is coming to town

He sees you when you're sleeping
He knows when you're awake
He knows if you've been bad or good
So be good for goodness sake!

O! You better watch out!
You better not cry
Better not pout
I'm telling you why
Santa Claus is coming to town
Santa Claus is coming to town

Henry Gillespie and J. Fred Coots

Deck the Halls

Deck the halls with boughs of holly,
Fa-la-la-la-la, la-la-la-la.
'Tis the season to be jolly,
Fa-la-la-la-la, la-la-la-la.

Don we now our gay apparel,
Fa-la-la, la-la-la, la-la-la.
Toll the ancient yule-tide carol,
Fa-la-la-la-la, la-la-la-la.

See the blazing yule before us,
Fa-la-la-la-la, la-la-la-la.
Strike the harp and join the chorus,
Fa-la-la-la-la, la-la-la-la.

Follow me in merry measure,
Fa-la-la-la-la, la-la-la-la.
While I tell of yuletide treasure.
Fa-la-la-la-la, la-la-la-la.

Fast away the old year passes,
Fa-la-la-la-la, la-la-la-la.
Hail the new year, lads and lasses,
Fa-la-la-la-la, la-la-la-la.

Sing we joyous, all together,
Fa-la-la-la-la, la-la-la-la.
heedless of the wind and weather,
Fa-la-la-la-la, la-la-la-la.

We Wish You a Merry Christmas

Chorus

We wish you a Merry Christmas,
We wish you a Merry Christmas,
We wish you a Merry Christmas
and a Happy New Year.

Good tidings we bring
to you and your king,
Good tidings for Christmas
and a Happy New Year.
Oh, bring us a figgy pudding,
Oh, bring us a figgy pudding,
Oh, bring us a figgy pudding
and a cup of good cheer.

Repeat Chorus

Christmas Fancies

When Christmas bells are swinging
Above the fields of snow,
We hear sweet voices ringing
From lands of long ago.
And etched on vacant places
Are half forgotten faces
Of friends we used to cherish
And loves we used to know –
When Christmas bells are swinging
Above the fields of snow.

Ella Wheeler Wilcox (1850–1919)

The Twelve Days of Christmas

On the first day of Christmas
My true love gave to me

A partridge in a pear tree.

On the second day of Christmas
My true love gave to me

Two turtledoves
And a partridge in a pear tree.

On the third day of Christmas
My true love gave to me

Three French hens
Two turtledoves
And a partridge in a pear tree.

On the fourth day of Christmas
My true love gave to me

Four calling birds
Three French hens
Two turtledoves
And a partridge in a pear tree.

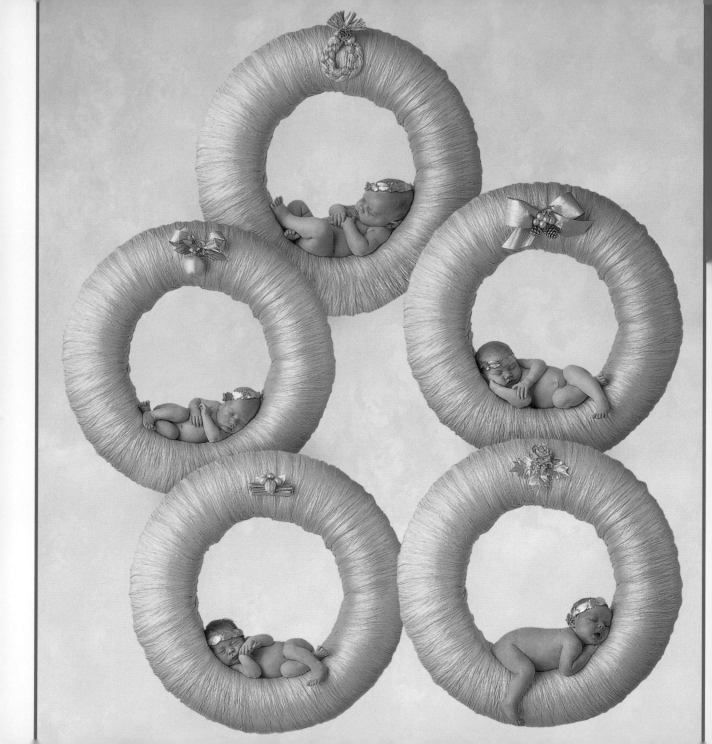

On the fifth day of Christmas

My true love gave to me

Five gold rings

Four calling birds

Three French hens

Two turtledoves

And a partridge in a pear tree.

On the sixth day of Christmas
My true love gave to me

Six geese a-laying
Five gold rings
Four calling birds
Three French hens
Two turtledoves
And a partridge in a pear tree.

On the seventh day of Christmas

My true love gave to me

Seven swans a-swimming

Six geese a-laying

Five gold rings

Four calling birds

Three French hens

Two turtledoves

And a partridge in a pear tree.

On the eighth day of Christmas
My true love gave to me

Eight maids a-milking
Seven swans a-swimming
Six geese a-laying
Five gold rings
Four calling birds
Three French hens
Two turtledoves
And a partridge in a pear tree.

On the ninth day of Christmas

My true love gave to me

Nine ladies dancing

Eight maids a-milking

Seven swans a-swimming

Six geese a-laying

Five gold rings

Four calling birds

Three French hens

Two turtledoves

And a partridge in a pear tree.

On the tenth day of Christmas
My true love gave to me

Ten lords a-leaping
Nine ladies dancing
Eight maids a-milking
Seven swans a-swimming
Six geese a-laying
Five gold rings
Four calling birds
Three French hens
Two turtledoves
And a partridge in a pear tree.

On the eleventh day of Christmas
My true love gave to me

Eleven pipers piping
Ten lords a-leaping
Nine ladies dancing
Eight maids a-milking
Seven swans a-swimming
Six geese a-laying
Five gold rings
Four calling birds
Three French hens
Two turtledoves
And a partridge in a pear tree.

On the twelfth day of Christmas

My true love gave to me

Twelve drummers drumming

Eleven pipers piping

Ten lords a-leaping

Nine ladies dancing

Eight maids a-milking

Seven swans a-swimming

Six geese a-laying

Five gold rings

Four calling birds

Three French hens

Two turtledoves

And a partridge in a pear tree.

On the twelfth day of Christmas

My true love gave to me

Twelve drummers drumming

Eleven pipers piping

Ten lords a-leaping

Nine ladies dancing

Eight maids a-milking

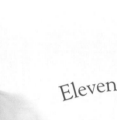

Seven swans a-swimming

Six geese a-laying

Five gold rings

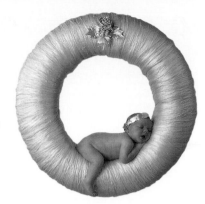

Four calling birds

Three French hens

Two turtledoves

And a partridge in a pear tree.

The Twelve Days of Christmas

1. On the first day of Christ-mas my true love gave to me a par-tridge___in a pear tree.

2. On the se-cond day of Christ-mas my true love gave to me two tur-tle-doves and a par-tridge___in a pear tree.

3. On the third day of Christ-mas my true love gave to me three French___hens, two tur-tle-doves and a par-tridge___in a pear tree.

4. On the fourth day of Christ-mas my true love gave to me four cal-ling birds, three French___hens, two tur-tle-doves and a

par - tridge＿＿in a pear tree. 5. On the fifth day of Christ - mas my

true love gave to me five gold＿＿ rings, four＿＿cal - ling birds,

three French hens, two＿＿tur - tle - doves and a par - tridge＿＿in a pear tree. 6. On the

sixth day of Christ-mas my true love gave to me | six geese a - lay - ing,
seventh | se - ven swans a - swim - ming, (to 6)
eighth | eight maids a - milk - ing, (to 7)
ninth | nine lad - ies dan - cing, (to 8)
tenth | ten lords a - leap - ing, (to 9)
elev-enth | elev - en pi - pers pi - ping, (to 10)
twelfth | twelve drum - mers drum - ming, (to 11)

five gold＿＿ rings, four＿＿ cal - ling birds,

three French hens, two＿＿ tur - tle doves and a

Six times   D.S.   Last time

par - tridge＿＿ in a pear tree. On the tree.

ANNE GEDDES ®

www.annegeddes.com

© 2006 Anne Geddes

First published in 2006 by Photogenique Publishers
(a division of Hachette Livre NZ Ltd)
4 Whetu Place, Mairangi Bay, Auckland, New Zealand

This edition published in North America in 2006
by Andrews McMeel Publishing, LLC
an Andrews McMeel Universal company
4520 Main Street, Kansas City, Missouri 64111

Produced by Kel Geddes
Printed in China by Midas Printing Limited, Hong Kong

ISBN-13: 978-0-7407-6245-1
ISBN-10: 0-7407-6245-1

www.andrewsmcmeel.com